LIVING IN A VAN: THE SMARTEST DECISION YOU MIGHT EVER MAKE

Bryan Westra

Ann Arbor, Michigan

Table of Contents

Course Notes:

Course Notes:

Course Notes:

Course Notes:

"Our values are simple: Namely, simple living; high thinking."

—Anonymous

Living In A Van: The Smartest Decision You Might Ever Make

About Living In A Van

Living in a van is something lots of individuals hope to achieve who embrace minimalism and simple living and high thinking principles. The main problem is that many have absolutely no clue how to begin or even what's involved in transitioning to this new way of life. An individual might feel owning a traditional home is the way to get started in life. Some might end up sacrificing and saving for that, while not knowing they are on the wrong path. It is essential to understand that owning a traditional home and living in a van are two entirely different ventures. We will review what precisely you need to do to live in a van and make the most of the experience.

Although it can help you to start residing in a small space, you initially need to make sure that living in a van is right for you. Residing in a small space is not meant for everybody, and you ought to think about that before proceeding (especially if you've grown accustomed to owning and possessing a lot of 'stuff'.

Before living in a van, it makes sense to analyze your daily practices. Then compare that against someone already ready to adhering to a minimalist lifestyle. You ought to investigate someone that is effectively doing that which you want to accomplish. Then see if you're reflecting what they achieve. This is a good starting place. Check out YouTube videos of people documenting their van living experiences too! This will help. The following are questions you ought to ask yourself:

Do you want to reduce your cost of living?

Do you want to save money?

Do you want to be free to travel and live where ever you desire?

These are certainly the type of obvious questions that someone who expects to live in a van should answer yes to. By replying to these particular questions with 'yes', that means that you maintain the personality type that would do well in living in a van.

Saving money and purchasing a van would probably not be the most difficult part of preparing. Preparing to live in a van can be a very long process that involves around six months of getting things in order, including your mindset. It is smart to become as ready as possible prior to day one of going for it and moving into your van.

The following are some tips to get you on your way:

-- Detaching from material possessions

Detaching from material possessions is so imperative because without doing that, you can feel trapped by the things you own and a prisoner confined to your domicile. This can result in being incapable of living in a van. There are a handful of virtues that individuals need to maintain in order to reside in a tiny space. So anyone with these virtues would engage in intentionally disengaging from material possessions regularly.

-- Living with less

Regardless of how much you prepare yourself to live in a van, it is indisputable that living with less is a must right off the bat. This is the reason it makes sense to practice living with less right now, before you jump into all the nitty gritty of the things you need to make happen.

-- Planning living in a van

The key to prospering with living in a van is dependent upon planning to live in a van, yet lots of individuals do not understand just how essential that really is! Through planning to live in a van, you can see to it that you're ready to live in a van from several vantage points.

Living in a van involves slightly more than getting up one afternoon to say, "Hey, I need to live in a van." Maybe it can be a starting step. However to gain some benefit with living in a van, you should initially prepare mentally.

Living In A Van - A Look Back

Understand you are not the first individual in the world that has had aspirations of living in a van. Really, there are thousands of people everywhere that wish to reside in a small space. The actual truth is that just a handful of them will actually make the commitment and accomplish it and follow-through.

Living in a van is not just a fleeting pastime, or like owning a traditional home. To become ready, you certainly need to become thrifty, conditioned to living with less, and free in your thinking. Then you are certainly ready to reside in a small space.

You've already begun a big step towards being ready to live in a van. Many individuals mess up for a legitimate reason. They frankly did not understand what precisely they were getting themselves into. Living in a van is truly something that needs you to become totally determined and prepared. Through looking ahead and making sure you are thrifty and conditioned for minimalist living, you are taking the first big step toward preparing.

You had recently asked yourself: "Do you want to reduce your cost of living?" Honestly, you had to ask that to yourself. Anyone who said "no" to that will be powerless to take one action to live in a van.

Additionally make sure you possess the staying power that living in a van would take. Do you want to reduce your cost of living? There would be a distinct difference between trusting something is a positive idea and actually doing it.

Undoubtedly, you would need a great deal of discipline to persevere.

Regardless of how far back you might care to look, you would discover that folks who are living in a van maintain one distinct thing in common: they knew precisely what they were getting into before taking the dive to live in their vans. They all acknowledged precisely what it was likely going to be like, what living in a van involved, and what was required of them to carry out their specific goals. When you understand precisely what it involves to live in a van, there is nothing to stop you!

Living in a van has a tangible aspect to it. Any action that you plan ahead of time will yield a better result. You'll discover the strength behind your mind will guide you to your goal.

Bear in mind that planning to live in a van is the number one method to insure your victory. In the event you begin feeling worn out, bear in mind that by planning living in a van in your legwork, you can be ready to defeat this challenge. Let's move along to brief you to what is required to live in a van.

Living In A Van In Everyday Life

Living in a van should be viewed as a way to live. This is something that you may integrate into your lifestyle in various ways. So during the six months briefing leading up to living in a van, you ought to analyze how residing in a small space can impact your lifestyle.

If you think back to when we initially started the quest of living in a van, you might recollect being presented with these questions:

Do you want to reduce your cost of living?

Do you want to save money?

Do you want to be free to travel and live where ever you desire?

These are questions that tap into attributes that establish if you were able to live in a van. These could be lifestyle choices. Assuming you responded "no" to these specific questions, you were not merely verifying that you were ready to live in a van, but also, you affirmed your lifestyle.

Definitely no one can ever say living in a van is easy. It is indisputable you must be thrifty and desire to have more by living with less to even contemplate living in a van. Just bear in mind that fulfilling activities require time and sacrifice. If realizing huge successes was as easy as snapping your fingers, everyone may be doing it.

In addition, someone needs to become focused on creating a better life for themselves. This is not just a trait that is required to live in a van, but also with other aspects of life.

Living in a van seriously takes loads more out of someone than one may think. Living in a van is not just something to achieve, it is also a whole lifestyle shift. It apparently involves a rare set of attributes to live in a van with confidence, knowing you've made the right decision for how you'll live your life.

To realize your goal, you might need to alter how you think. Basically there's a clear-cut state of mind that anyone who may live in a van would share. Firstly, someone who may live in a van should be unquestionably thrifty and this means pinching pennies. This is an example of an attribute that would influence other areas in your life.

Be sure to analyze what is required before living in a van. This is precisely what can be advantageous in different areas of life. Living with less, detaching from material possessions and planning living in a van ought to be viewed as activities

[31]

that transcend residing in a small space such as a tiny home. While we are discussing this as being tailored to living in a van, all of it can impact other areas of life.

The most serious individuals would see their specific goals through. You can become one of these individuals. If you allow yourself to become free, you find the quest is an exciting one and kudos for taking the plunge!

Why Live In A Van

Living in a van has become an amazingly desired activity among individuals everywhere. There are endless reasons to live in a van, which is the reason lots of individuals try to endeavor it. Living in a van can be done to save money for the future, to promote minimalism, or to be where you want to be when you want to be there. While the probable intentions for living in a van are endless, there could be a handful that stick out as the most common.

Save Money For The Future

Living in a van to save money for the future is a good reason to reside in a small space. Every time you have a clear-cut reason to live in a van, that makes the aspiration more significant. Then when you finally commit to adhering to a minimalist lifestyle, it should feel sweeter.

Promote Minimalism

A typical reason that lots of individuals elect to live in a van is to promote minimalism. This is a

[34]

perfect reason to live in a van as well. A minimalist is someone who sheds excess in order not to be weighed down. They adhere to the philosophy that less is best and anything more than a must is a problem they don't need or want. Letting go of your material possessions may seem at first a real challenge (mentally at least). Most people who decide to live in a van, despite their views on minimalism, find after some time they never think about those items they gave up (sacrificed). This is because things don't always make us happy; sometimes they hold us back from experiencing the freedom and joy that comes with having less. It is about de-cluttering your life so you experience the thrill of being surrounded with less things that may very likely be the root cause of many of your stresses.

Be Where You Want To Be When You Want To Be There

Another reason that people choose to live in a van is to be where they want to be when they want to be there. Residing in a small space is a difficult feat. Once you live in a van successfully, you would also have a unique relationship with others that have also lived in a van. There are whole communities of van dwellers who call themselves 'boondockers' who regularly get together over a season to share the freedom that comes with living out of a van, whilst enjoying community with other like-minded individuals who share the same values.

Overall, living in a van can bring a big sense of achievement to your way of living, and with good reason. Priming for this is an exciting commitment, which is the definite reason that some individuals choose to reside in a small space. In addition, living in a van can also offer you a clear outlook on life. And once you live in a van, you should learn that you can achieve just about anything else in this world. That is, if you open your mind and try it. The intentions to live in a van are absolutely different from one person to the next. So ultimately, you ought to endeavor this for your own individual reasons.

Things To Do Before Living In A Van

A guide full of stuff to achieve before living in a van can easily fill up lots of full-length books. Living in a van is difficult. That is apparently reflected through the large amount of guidance material existent to anyone attempting to reside in a small space. Despite this reality, there are several proven methods that every minimalist van dweller ought to make to their regimented schedule. It also, doesn't matter how experienced that minimalist van dweller is; you ought to make it work. The most essential factor to keep in mind is that you need to prepare, both physically and mentally.

"Camping out is the key," some van dwellers argue. You would never be ready to live in a van if you only work on preparing a little bit every now and then. Adhere to a regimented schedule and stick to it. It is acceptable to take a day off every so often, but you ought to be pretty determined on preparing everyday. Camping out regularly can encourage you in a slew of ways. You can even begin to believe differently. You'll get a reality check in small doses which can help you build up your resistance to 'resistance'.

You will be better ready for any challenge because you would become stronger. You will definitely think more positive about yourself in general. Remember that you're a thrifty person, and you ought to make the necessary adjustments to reflect that. Get in the routine of camping out so you are typically feeling detached from your home and feeling one with your surroundings.

Equally essential as camping out is traveling afar. When you observe individuals who have efficiently lived in a van, you can see that they typically travel afar. That is because they understand the value of this practice. Traveling afar results in enjoying new experiences. It is already known that traveling afar also can see new sights. Keep in mind, you should have a back-up plan (contingency plan in place) in case things go wrong. That can foster a sense of safety by having a plan 'b' to fall back on should you need to fall back.

Crowds of individuals would agree that they could be meeting different types of people, merely by traveling afar. That can get your mind on structuring your daily activities to live in a van. When residing in a small space, that should encourage you to bear in mind the reason you were doing this all to begin with. You will also remember the tips and techniques have helped you in the past.

Another great benefit that a minimalist van dweller has is when they reduce possessions. They are living with less clutter. Being ready to live in a van is important. But that can be futile if you were incapable of living in a van for a long time. Reducing possessions has a slew of positive effects that go beyond residing in a small space. Reducing possessions results in living with less clutter and living with less attachment to things.

There are a handful of additional considerations to bear in mind when you're reducing possessions. Be content with less things holding your back from living a freer life. That can directly produce a more positive result so you can feel free to exist without the responsibility of ownership. In addition, reducing possessions can encourage you to live with less fear of loss. And by keeping a positive point-of-view, it will help you on any discouraging moments you might experience. Think about what you could do to enhance your life, and grow from there. A positive point-of-view can make a huge difference when you're living in a van.

Typical Mistakes Made While You Live In A Van

[45]

Yes, there could be a few activities that you will not want to endeavor experiencing while residing in a small space. While every new minimalist van dweller would make a handful of mistakes, there are a couple in particular that you want to prevent experiencing at all costs.

Do not give away everything you own. That can cause you to fall back in all of your efforts. Why would someone invest all that effort only to reverse what they have done? This is what takes place when you give away everything you own. Many people who have given away everything, feel terrified after a week of living in a van under duress. For example, if you are sick, living in a van can be a nightmarish experience. You may want to invest in a hotel room for a couple days, should this happen at a severe level. Imagine being sick, puking, snot rags everywhere, the air is stuffy and humidity is prevalent, your breathing is not so good, and you are feeling feverish... How does this make you feel about not having anything familiar to comfort you— like your old possessions and memorabilia? See what I mean! It can be tormenting psychologically, so before committing 100% just commit to placing your belonging in storage until you are absolutely certain, after some time has passed, and you're mentally ready to part with those items. You probably won't miss them – but, who's to say you won't, right?

There's something that can help you prevent certain mistakes from occurring. If you have been residing in a small space for a while, set a bit of time off to split up the legwork involved.

In addition, do not tell people your plans who might hinder them. That is the other essential issue that any minimalist van dweller ought to avoid. While there are lots of options for residing in a small space, reflecting on these recommendations can produce a really positive ending no matter what. Provided you're sensible with your activities and pursue your training, then you would be ready to adhere to a minimalist lifestyle.

Rules to Consider While Living In A Van

Priming to live in a van definitely needs someone to be thrifty, concentrated on building wealth for themselves, and a free spirit. At times these attributes can be commanded out of someone when certain procedures are set in motion. This section will investigate those procedures that have been designed purposefully to advance those precise attributes.

Preparing your consciousness for the tough task of living in a van is time-consuming, and you'd most likely be spending close to six months making preparations. This would offer you enough time to ingrain these particular procedures in your regiment.

Just remain alert to your surroundings. This will help you be calibrated to anything out of the ordinary that may pose a threat to your well-being. It is one of many results that this guideline will produce. In addition, you will feel detached from your home, particularly when the moment comes to actually live in your van.

Also, bear in mind that folks who effectively travel afar will typically have a back-up plan in case things go wrong. It is amazing how these trouble-free guidelines can be such a key part in a bigger goal. When you see yourself as someone set on growing your wealth by living thrifty, then you can find it pretty simple to adopt these procedures into your disciplined schedule. In addition, if you actually decide to have a back-up plan in case things go wrong, then it can foster a sense of safety by having a plan 'b' to fall back on. All of these point are important for you to contemplate and rationalize sensibly.

Let us remember this goal of reducing possessions. That would require yet another degree of energy during the period of preparation, but it will be worth it. During the time you are working on living with less attachment to things and living with less fear of loss, you should be content with less things holding your back from living a freer life. Through making sure that you uphold this mindset, you can feel free to exist without the responsibility of ownership.

Living in a van isn't like owning a traditional home. While anybody can look to reside in a small space, it takes someone who is free and thrifty to actually realize the objective of living in a van.

Once you're totally serious, you can achieve anything! Think back to the following questions:

Do you want to reduce your cost of living?

Do you want to save money?

Do you want to be free to travel and live where ever you desire?

You proved you were thrifty, wealth conscious, and free spirited by saying "yes" to each of those three questions. Every moment you are living in your van, these attributes would help you grow in prosperity. If you apply these main guidelines, and you camp out, travel afar from time-to-time, and reduce possessions slowly, in turn you'd become a van dweller in no time!

What You Need to Know Before Living In A Van

We considered several of the distinct habits that someone who expects to live in a van ought to consider carrying out. Now that you have realized the practices of someone desiring to live in a van, the likelihood is that several practices are integrated into your daily life already. You ought to investigate how you can propagate these choices into a greater part of your lifestyle.

[57]

This can make briefing to live in a van an easy transformation.

After all, preparing to achieve the utmost objective can cause you to make several transformations in your life. Your openness to transforming yourself can be the determining factor in how rapidly you achieve your objectives.

Are you ready to live with less? Are you ready to detach from material possessions and plan to live in a van? These were only a handful of habits to prepare you toward the quest of living in a van. If that looks distressing, do not be alarmed. We have several recommendations pertaining to achieving your ambitions.

Don't skip through the preparatory phases.

At times it looks as if the preparatory phases can be disregarded. Perhaps you can feel you can overcome without carrying out preparations like living with less. There could most likely come a point after beginning the groundwork of living in a van where you would experience a task just like camping out. Assuming you finished the preparatory phases now, you would experience a much easier time achieving your ambitions.

Investing a pre-determined amount of time merely to hone in on the subsidiary preparations is best. That would cause the last segment of your quest to be smoother. Conclusively, you can be fully ready to live in a van after the preparation.

Don't call it quits if you mess up preparing.

Despite how significant your effort can be, expect problems. Rather than striving for perfection, look at following the preparatory phases for the majority of the time. This would offer you a buffer to mess up the steps periodically. If you anticipate swaying from perfection periodically, that can prevent you from quitting throughout the time you stumble from the steps of living in a van.

Buy a van. Owning a van before you commit to this lifestyle change will help you become acquainted with the small interior space you'd eventually be living in. It will also let you practice camping out overnight in your van on small stints and vacations. You can also get a sense of what you'll be able to bring with you in the van, once you commit to living full time in your van.

That might sound like an indisputable thing to achieve when you were briefing to live in a van. Nonetheless it is remarkable how some individuals mess up getting fitting equipment beforehand. This is an easy tip to look at. Don't make the biggest misstep of rushing through these imperative preparations.

Get mentally prepared. Mindset is everything. If you want to adopt this lifestyle, you must be mentally prepare for it, less it freaks you out and you stop altogether with it. Once you are 100% on board with living with little, living in a confined space, and operating daily out of your van, you are all set to start this journey.

Whether you're attempting to carry out a material aspiration or something that involves more mental energy, your head guides what you do. That is the reason, it is essential to train yourself toward the project ahead. When the mind is equipped with the project ahead, that makes carrying out the work quicker. What we accomplish begins with an idea. Plant positive ideas in your head, and your quest to live in a van would be really underway.

When you consider calling it quits, do not.

It is typical to feel discouraged when things become difficult. If living in a van was painless, anyone would be doing it. The truth is that living in a van involves a bit of effort and deliberate action. The benefits could be undoubtedly fulfilling. Although you may venture to call it quits when things become difficult, do not. Don't call it quits because you can accomplish this!

Alleviate the opinions you have relating to living in a van.

With TV, the Internet and social networking so uncontrollable in our lifestyle, it is probable to have preconceived ideas about living in a van. Much of your opinions relating to living in a van are not entirely correct. Assume difficult work and sacrifice to accomplish your goal of living in a van. Despite how you look at it, a thrifty and prosperity conscious individual can do well at living in a van. If you were incapable to identify yourself as wealth conscious and thrifty now, do not be alarmed. These attributes are bolstered and you must develop yourself to become thrifty and prosperity conscious.

Get a gym membership. Gyms will give you a place to work out, plus provide you with a shower anytime you want to shower. You may even be able to stealth camp in the parking lot of a 24-hour gym (e.g., Planet Fitness / Gold's Gym).

While living in a van begins with a quest with you, there is the material aspect that is similarly essential. While your will is in a proper place, you actually have to work the material steps. These recommendations were so essential because that draws upon the material aspect of living in a van.

These are some specific habits that can prepare you for your experience. You ought to prepare to work for about six months to reside in a small space. Prior to when the six months starts, you ought to be reflecting these specific suggestions. A commitment involves a moment to set into action. It begins with a promise in your mind. Manage a diary to track your progression and that can encourage you to continue on track.

If you go off track, get right back on. Living in a van is a quest and periodically you may go off track. The essential thing is that you bounce right back on! Most importantly, make sure that you're basking in your experience. Anyone that aspires to live in a van expects to bring in some mental gratification from it. In addition feed off the acknowledgement you bring in along the way when you eventually adhering to a minimalist lifestyle!

The Easiest Way To Live In A Van

While there are hundreds of guides available related to living in a van, there is one message they all relay: the preparation phase is very essential. A standard period of time to reside in a small space is around six months. Priming for so long offers you the essential energy to live in a van.

Before your preparation phase commences, there are activities that you need to achieve. We will cover some trouble-free instructions that will put you into the right mindset for this big undertaking, thus urging you to get where you need to be to productively live in a van. One of those activities you need to make happen the instant you begin briefing is to live with less. In addition, detaching from material possessions and planning living in a van both chip in to get your life ready for living in a van.

Preparing for at least six months before you live in a van is very essential, and can't be overemphasized. That allows you to totally prepare. In addition, it offers you these three beneficial habits required for living in a van. You should discover that camping out, traveling afar, and reducing possessions will insure that you expend your greatest effort possible.

When you leave out these particular guidelines, you can forego feeling detached from your home, feeling one with your surroundings, and priming yourself for constant change in your living space. These results all stem from the preparation phase.

If you invest in residing in a small space, then you would discover that it is certainly easier than you may expect. Proper preparation allows you to become completely ready. This results in priming yourself for constant change in your living space, meeting different types of people and living with less fear of loss. These benefits allow you to productively live in a van. That being said, do not merely scurry through all the training because all these benefits are similarly essential.

At times, when observing people who productively live in a van, it can be easy to feel that they maintain magical energy or know some special trick that permits them to become a van dweller. However, there is no secret. Living in a van only needs someone who is thrifty, wealthy and free. Through making the time to see to it that your efforts are working, you would be ready to live in a van at a fast pace.

That may sound like a long time to invest, but realistically six months quickly tends to fly by. It is typical to think that way, particularly while preparing for an adventure as big as living in a van. Provided you proceed to invest the right effort, you can be living in a van in no time. Living in a van can be difficult. However, by preparing the most effective way, you can be sure to conquer it!

Living In A Van For Free

At times, individuals feel it is cost prohibitive to live in a van. It's generally the opposite. You can really reside in a small space for next to nothing. When you're looking to reside in a small space, the important thing to make happen is to get started with a clear mentality. In other words, strip from your mind all preconceived notions of what all the preparation period for living in a van is expected to be like.

There are only three basic instructions that can help you stabilize your aspirations of living in a van with your wallet. Don't spend money on expensive meals. You can save a lot of money by investing in a cooler to contain your less costly store bought food from discounters. Practice eating foods that are easy to prepare and which are a healthy choice. This will keep you healthy and sound while living in a van. When you deliberately concentrate on options that do not require a great deal of money, then you permit your consciousness to hone in on the things you need to be carrying out.

Also consider, camping out, traveling afar and reducing possessions are actions that are ultimately important and do not need a lot of money.

There are many different preparations you can also try, in order to squander less money. Budget your travel expenses. Buy gas when it is down price-wise and travel less to save on gasoline/petrol. Also, ensure that you are not buying things you do not need (too much will clutter up your van and invade your small living space). You do not need to invest a lot of money to reside in a small space. Everytime you deliberately put your emotions aside relating to money, then you ought to discover lots of free options that are possibly better versus the more cost prohibitive ones. That is an easy alternative when your objectives are the focus.

During the time you're reducing possessions, achieve it with a mindset to save cash. Get oil changes at regular intervals and learn how to fix minor repairs. You can learn about your vehicle by watching YouTube videos, through online resources, and by talking to knowledgeable professionals. The more you can do for yourself, the less you'll spend hiring out other people's services. During the time you're living in a van you do not need to squander cash on overly expensive services when there are free choices that work equally as great. Many individuals were living in a van before lots of of the more expensive services were made. If they didn't need it, then you would not either.

The key thing that you ought to do is to consistently be focused on your specific goals. Most importantly, traveling afar, reducing possessions and camping out are a handful of the best activities that you ought to be focused upon. Through typically evaluating decisions through the filter of your specific goals, you would recognize what costs could be luxuries that you do not truly need.

When you invest the time in preparing, you would feel detached from your home, which is one of the important results for living in a van. Camping out doesn't entail investing a lot of cash. Camping out requires getting in the habit of traveling afar. And many times it might sound undoubtedly expensive, but realistically you can travel afar without going bankrupt. Traveling afar helps you to see new sights which also doesn't entail a large amount of cash. It can be achieved very inexpensively.

Reducing possessions is a different thing that you ought to be focused on because it is really important for someone who expects to live in a van. While there might be expensive choices that sound good, you ought to naturally reduce possessions without necessarily having to pay much for it.

Ultimately, if you'd be determined on your objectives, then you ought to prevent unnecessary spending to accomplish your ambition of living in a van. There are typically choices available that are low in cost. Comprehending how your emotions affect your spending would allow you to manage costs when you're working towards living in a van.

Living In A Van - Step by Step

At this point, it is clear what kind of person it takes to productively live in a van. We have also learned of which attributes that someone definitely needs in order to reside in a small space. So right now, we can now get started with the things we are set to accomplish.

Undoubtedly, the first step is confirming that you are absolutely camping out because this can establish your readiness to live in a van. You ought to think of camping out as this: no person can realistically reside in a small space without camping out. It is completely impossible - that is exactly how imperative this step is.

Camping out is also imperative if you hope to become successful. That can also result with you feeling detached from your home and feeling one with your surroundings. Once you begin camping out, you'd have a great deal to gain and nothing to lose!

In addition, traveling afar is needed to reside in a small space. There are apparently many benefits for this. Enjoying new experiences, though, is known as the most pertinent great benefit of living in a van. Without enjoying new experiences, you can expect that it can become extremely difficult to productively reside in a small space.

Traveling afar also provides extraordinary benefits in unique ways other than living in a van. That can help you see new sights and meet different types of people. Also seeing new sights is equally essential whether you were living in a van or not. So, you should look at executing any method that gets you seeing new sights.

You should be ready for living in a van in at least six months once you begin camping out, particularly if you're traveling afar from time to time to experience what it's like to be far away from everything familiar to you. Generally, six months is the average period of time that people spend getting ready to live in a van. Consider these averages when you're setting your timelines.

One other factor that is required to help you become successful with living in a van is reducing possessions. You do not need to hone in on reducing possessions until the latter part of your preparations, however definitely do not eliminate it altogether. Reducing possessions ought to guide you to live with less clutter, and would be beneficial for your preparations. That also helps you to live with less attachment to things and live with less fear of loss, which in turn helps you to live in a van.

Conclusively, you'd be ready to live in a van by camping out, traveling afar and reducing possessions. It generally takes six months of the preparation period to become totally prepared. But, that period of time would go by really rapidly. If you select a date to initialize your training and mark six months later, then it will allow your mind to see that timeframe as the preparatory phase. At that point, you'd be prepared to hone in on camping out, and traveling afar. Afterwards, you'd discover that your entire spirit is totally prepared to live in a van!

Strategies To Living In A Van

Once you choose to live in a van, you may become curious in certain tactics to confirm that you're addressing your specific goals in a prudent way. There are clear-cut requirements to living in a van efficiently. These requirements are relating to qualities and attributes someone holds.

Residing in a small space definitely needs someone to become devoted.

So, someone that is spendthrift, or otherwise spender, might probably not become as effective as they could really be. These attributes belong to someone who might have said "no" when presented with the question:

Do you want to reduce your cost of living?

If you hope to live in a van, several attributes are needed. Being thrifty is an indisputable must. If you hope to carry out your aspiration of living in a van and ultimately become a van dweller, then you would need to become wealthy.

Anyone can say that they hope to live in a van. However, living in a van is a big step above owning a traditional home. One doesn't take a lot of scheduling, whereas preparation is definitely essential to the overall success of the other.

Living with less is a core tactic with preparing to live in a van. Though, individuals usually misjudge the value of that. The truth remains that living with less is essential with residing in a small space. On a separate note, living in a van also benefits all other aspects in our daily lives.

Detaching from material possessions is also required when it comes to preparing to live in a van. It makes perfect sense just how essential detaching from material possessions is to reside in a small space.

Lastly, planning living in a van is key to see to it you are successful in living in a van. That can sound like a simple action, but it isn't unheard of to stumble from it. So, keep planning living in a van while staying focused on realizing your aspiration.

Residing in a small space and subsequently living in a van to become a van dweller, can encourage you now and after your deliberate actions. You should discover feeling detached from your home, enjoying new experiences, and living with less clutter each stem from you living in a van. Residing in a small space is pursued by lots of individuals because they understand the benefits that living in a van comes with.

Once you integrate those tactics in order to live in a van, you'd discover your present virtues significantly enhanced. Any thrifty person would

become more thrifty. Any wealthy
person would be more wealthy. And
any free person would become more
free. This is the reason there is
definitely no better moment to start
than right now!

Tips To Live In A Van Better

Once you commit to living in a van, there are various activities that you can try to reside in a small space better. Following are a handful of tips that can result in living in a van:

- Camping out has already been considered in complete depth, and that is rather essential when you're living in a van. Please be sure that you be calibrated to anything out of the ordinary that may pose a threat. In addition, make it a habit to Remain alert to your surroundings. That doesn't only affect living in a van, it actually affects your way of living in general.

- By now, we ought to understand the value of traveling afar. This is an essential step toward preparing to live in a van. That may be difficult, and the best method to overcome the challenge is to Have a back-up plan in case things go wrong. This can foster a sense of safety by having a plan 'b' to fall back on.

- It can be difficult to be focused on reducing possessions, however this is essential for the goal of living in a van. It makes sense to Be content with less things holding your back from living a freer life. This can feel free to exist without the responsibility of ownership.

Living in a van can guide you to secure a great deal of benefits, particularly as more time passes.

When you live in a van, you might experience the following benefits:

- Bear in mind feeling detached from your home can take place more often as long as you're camping out.

- Camping out can also help you feel one with your surroundings.

- Traveling afar can result in enjoying new experiences.

- In addition, traveling afar helps with seeing new sights.

- As you work to reduce possessions, you should discover that you are living with less attachment to things.

- Reducing possessions also will live with less attachment to things.

Residing in a small space offers a great deal of direct benefits, a handful of of which we have successfully considered. , meeting different types of people, and priming yourself for constant change in your living space all occur when you're camping out, traveling afar, and reducing possessions. Residing in a small space requires carrying out all of these particular things and celebrating the benefits that follow. In addition, below are a few additional tips:

- Don't spend money on expensive meals. You can save a lot of money by investing in a cooler to contain your less costly store bought food. Practice eating foods that are easy to prepare and which are a healthy choice. This will keep you healthy and sound while living in a van.

- Budget your travel expenses. Buy gas when it is down price-wise and travel less to save on gasoline/petrol. Also, ensure that you are not buying things you do not need (too much will clutter up your van and invade your small living space).

- Get oil changes at regular intervals and learn how to fix minor repairs. You can learn about your vehicle by watching YouTube videos, through online resources, and by talking to knowledgeable professionals. The more you can do for yourself, the less you'll spend hiring out other people's services.

Once you heed the advice contained here, you'd be on the path to reside in a small space. Be sure to allow six months to prepare. Having a convenient amount of time to prepare is key.

Any instructions that are noted here present a starting point. Once looking at this information, you'd have an understanding of what it involves to live in a van. Take the initiative to add your individual reflections and create new recommendations to encourage you be successful.

The Best System For Living In A Van

There could be thousands of systems existent to individuals thinking more about living in a van, and they all proclaim to be the easiest. In reality, several of these particular systems, that you might find online, insure more positive benefits. Nonetheless, the victory of living in a van depends upon each person and their point-of-view towards planning. A good minimalist van dweller can be a good minimalist van dweller despite what the circumstances. Equally, a bad minimalist van dweller can continue to feel worse regardless if they are living in a van as a novice, or are more experienced in their craft. Living in a van is a mental activity equally as much as it is a physical one.

Over your six months of briefing leading up to the big moment, you should feel pretty busy planning in advance. Not only will residing in a small space physically challenge you, but also it also stimulates your brain. In regards to planning your overall plan, multi-faceted footwork is essential. There could be thousands of tools handy to help see the particulars of living in a van. Though, your individual intuition should be more optimal versus any tool. After all, you understand your body and state of mind like no one else. Apply that knowledge to calculate your goal and do not ignore your intuition because it is not likely to wrongfully guide you.

We pre-determined that the normal amount of time someone prepares to live in a van is six months. So, you ought to be generous while planning your time. Also consider, you understand your body better than anyone. If you need additional time, do not pressure yourself attempting to attain your aspiration in precisely six months. Do the math and determine the time you need. Lastly, alter your objectives accordingly.

During the time you make preparations to live in a van, you may find additional individuals that could be attempting to carry out the exact objective. Also consider, they are possibly working on a separate timeframe than you. So, do not get caught up challenging their agenda or techniques if it doesn't work with your daily rhythm. This is precisely how many people get worn out and finally give up. You've recently begun the first big step. So, continue at your own pace. One other bad idea is to make reckless decisions to alter your timeframes inappropriately. Start out slow and gradually invest more effort toward your goal as your preparations progress. This ascertains you'd become totally ready to live in a van.

While these tactics detailed here are not foolproof, they are the best starting points for novices attempting to live in a van. There are absolutely a great deal of recommendations that you can adopt to fit your preparation period, seeing that you know your state of mind. Apply the knowledge, and the plan produced here to get out there and finally live in a van! If you're sensible with how you spend your time, and apply the material here to calculate a workable plan, then you'd be a great minimalist van dweller in no time!

Do's and Don'ts of Living In A Van

Any dream of living in a van can be exhilarating and frightening. The legendary hippies from the 60's and 70's is a big progression in any minimalist van dweller's routine. At first that might sound beyond reach. Nonetheless, with the right training and preparation, living in a van can be conquered by anyone. Similar to any demanding challenge, living in a van can be conquered in a slew of ways. These are several things that every minimalist van dweller ought to (and ought to not) think of:

Before Living In A Van

While your challenge is living in a van, there could be various considerations that every minimalist van dweller ought to accomplish beforehand. This can insure that living in a van is not an impossible challenge.

DO Live With Less

If you want to live in a van, you should be investing sufficient time briefing. This can completely encourage you to live with less clutter and live with less attachment to things.

DON'T Give Away Everything You Own

It may be easy to neglect granting your schedule time off from briefing. However, the time of rest allows your mind to consider the aspiration of living in a van. Give your schedule time to consider achieving your ambitions so you avoid fatigue.

DO Detach From Material Possessions

The preparatory phases to living in a van is essential and by executing this painless suggestion of detaching from material possessions, you can be carrying out what you could to prepare.

DON'T Tell People Your Plans Who Might Hinder Them

If you miss every milestones in the heart of your legwork, that should not adversely influence your overall goal provided you invest the effort to bounce back on track. Avoid the tendency to expands your training disproportionately, because doing so can cause you to lose momentum.

While Living In A Van

DO Camp Out

Recognize what you can accomplish. Set your goal accordingly. By executing this suggestion, you can feel detached from your home and feel one with your surroundings. In addition, you can also prime yourself for constant change in your living space.

DON'T Forget To Prepare For The Weather Conditions (e.g., Extreme Temperatures, Ventilation In The Hot Summer Months)

The most experienced minimalist van dweller would be capable of live in a van quicker. That is because they might maintain personal experience. Rescue your energy and avoid analyzing yourself with a different minimalist van dweller and compare your progression only with yourself.

DO Travel Afar

This is an essential suggestion. By following this suggestion in your routine, you can feel detached from your home and feel one with your surroundings. In addition, you can prime yourself for constant change in your living space.

DON'T Get Caught Living In Your Van By The Authorities (Check The Laws, Because Some Places It Is Illegal To Camp Overnight In Your Vehicle)

There is no reason to test theories pertaining to living in a van. These are clear-cut instructions of what you should and should not try in order to do well and eventually adhering to a minimalist lifestyle.

After Living In A Van

After briefing to live in a van, remember, your quest is not complete! Following are a handful do's, and don'ts, to recognize once you accomplish the goal:

DO Take What You Learned Into Your Future Situations And Benefit From Them

DON'T Judge Yourself

DO Continue Living Simple

DON'T Resort Back To Old Habits That May No Longer Serve You

These are a handful of relatively easy tips to follow while living in a van. Appreciate the quest and bear in mind that the quest is yours!

How Living In A Van Will Change You

Living in a van isn't for the faint of heart. It may become incredibly difficult and the project does not get easier. Nonetheless, if you can brave the project to the journey's end, you may discover you are not the same personality type that you were before you began. Regardless of how well you train, something relating to solely attempting to live in a van provides so many advantages.

For example, you learn how to live in a van. Whether you overcome or fail, maintaining awareness of how to prepare is valuable to know. Regardless of the wealth of help and knowledge that you may discover online or within self-help books, attempting to live in a van provides unique insights into how the various strategies work. This kind of insight not only results in maintaining awareness of yourself better, but also gives you much needed information for other endeavors.

Metaphorically, living in a van proves how fully committed you are.

Living in a van is a desire that lots of people maintain, but barely a few maintain the dedication and focus to compete. Living in a van proves your sacrifice in the eyes of others, but also it demonstrates it to yourself. The guts and the willpower it involves to complete residing in a small space should not go away once you carry out your feat. Rather, they would remain a part of you.

Living in a van helps your brain by showing you have what it takes to adhering to a minimalist lifestyle. Living in a van also expands brainpower. Once you live in a van, you might be astonished by how you have gotten to this point both intellectually and physically. You can be feeling these advantageous effects for lots of years.

Conclusively, living in a van offers you bragging rights. With that said, not only can you share the exhilarating details of living in a van, with your close friends, but you can share the stages of preparation. Alternatively, you learn what you could be capable of. Living in a van involves a lot of courage, and knowing you have what it takes to endeavor something so difficult.

Living in a van unquestionably is extremely challenging, but it transforms you in lots of ways. It is no wonder that only a handful of people do well with living in a van. You could be showing yourself and the world that you maintain the skills and insight to endeavor some greater things in life!

Living In A Van - The Lifestyle

It is completely clear that individuals who want to live in a van come in all shapes and sizes. Nonetheless no matter your skill level, there are a handful of considerations that are typical among the individuals that want to live in a van. The reason a lot of individuals who live in a van maintain that vibe is because they all have a lifestyle with parallel values. This will not mean such people live parallel lives, because that would be impossible, and wrong. People who live in a van come from all walks of life. While such people may not share everything in common, there could be a handful of lifestyle traits and choices that they all share.

Obviously the lifestyle involves living with less. Without that, living in a van would feel cumbersome. Nonetheless, living with less is not strictly tailored to only living in a van. In addition, the lifestyle involves detaching from material possessions and planning living in a van. Residing in a small space can require camping out and traveling afar. The truth is that residing in a small space is an investment. In addition, reducing possessions may lead to all kinds of unexpected benefits.

Because of that, some individuals who venture to live in a van, especially folks that are steadfast, can immediately recognize these extra advantages. These benefits do not develop exclusively from camping out, either. After spending so much effort in planning your everyday life to live in a van, all individuals would see themselves unconsciously making better everyday choices within other aspects of life. People who have live in a van might discover that they could be able to feel detached from your home and feel one with your surroundings. While that isn't a miraculous talent that you can gain the instant you choose to live in a van, that is one thing that can gradually include itself in your lifestyle the more you prepare to reside in a small space.

These benefits are greater, but it can become undoubtedly easy to become swept away without even knowing it. If you maintain lots of friends that also would like to live in a van, you might discover that a handful of them never concentrate on anything else but living in a van. As with any life choice, a little careful moderation is required.

As you train for living in a van, you should discover that these particular lifestyle transformations are occuring in your life. Camping out and traveling afar makes sense in lots of ways, and subsequently, you would feel detached from your home and enjoy new experiences. The lifestyle is very hard, but it is unquestionably worth it. If you tough it all out, living in a van and the associated lifestyle can make your way of living better in various ways.

Is Living In A Van Right For You?

People who choose to live in a van are really steadfast. There are lots of qualities in life that can't be faked. You can't fake a job evaluation, or the results of an exam in school. Equally, you can't fake living in a van. You frankly can't live in a van without a little preparation. Residing in a small space involves someone to become thrifty and steadfast. That involves six months of preparing vigilantly.

As you are planning your lifestyle to live in a van, make sure that you do not give away everything you own. In addition, do not look to tell people your plans who might hinder them. Preparation involves time and it cannot be rushed. By rushing through the preparation period, you would not truly be preparing and it can be presumed that you faked your efforts through the steps. Doing things the right way would allow you to maintain longevity toward your results.

Living in a van ought to become quite exhilarating and offers a sense of achievement that you can cherish for years. Living in a van is a challenge. Whether you could be just starting or are totally experienced, there are rational pros and cons of living in a van.

There are even more advantages of living in a van and the biggest one is that it can offer you a sense of pride and achievement. Residing in a small space is a difficult activity. Living in a van is something that might typically remind you of your sacrifice and offer you a sense of satisfaction for even trying this activity.

Another great benefit of living in a van is that it improves your scheduling skills because you certainly need to prepare how you can move forward to actually adhering to a minimalist lifestyle. So once you choose to live in a van, you might learn a great deal about planning and staying focused.

There are indisputable benefits to living in a van. It is probably not as easy as it looks. There may be a handful of restrictions that you might need to rise above, like the huge amount of time required to plan. You ought to offer yourself six months, and make a total commitment. Do not look to plan in bits and pieces. Devotion and sincere effort would eventually allow you to adhering to a minimalist lifestyle.

This would offer you a bit of insight to establish if living in a van is right for you. Undoubtedly, living in a van definitely needs someone to become thrifty, wealthy and free. When you see yourself as the personality type with these particular attributes, you might be totally prepared to adhering to a minimalist lifestyle.

The most essential thing to be mindful of is there are definitely no shortcuts. People who have recently live in a van understand how much sacrifice is essential. You ought to heed your inner voice, which would guide you through the steps to living in a van.

Benefits of Living In A Van

Every time you reside in a small space, there are generally some important activities that you have to achieve. You certainly need to camp out, travel afar, and reduce possessions. These three activities do not only help anyone out with living in a van, they furthermore bring other advantages to life. Residing in a small space is something that has made countless people everywhere feel better about themselves.

People who were camping out might recognize slight transformations with their inner well-being. These individuals furthermore feel ready to tackle more in life. Priming in advance allows you to become stronger versus what you were in the past. This allows you to take on more than you could do before, and not lose energy as easily. It all benefits you, and that furthermore benefits you in your daily life.

You have recently identified yourself as a thrifty and wealthy personality type. Each free individual is characteristically equipped to live in a van.

Individuals travel afar when they plan to live in a van. Obviously, traveling afar has various benefits aside from merely enjoying new experiences and seeing new sights. You would also discover that you can meet different types of people. All this can make you feel better on a daily basis.

Residing in a small space also results in living with less clutter. That results from reducing possessions, especially spread over a longer term of time. In addition, that comes with tons of additional benefits. For example, you can live with less attachment to things. In addition you can live with less fear of loss.

Living in a van is an action where anyone can typically improve themselves through the preparation period. While preparing may be up to six months, that means that you would most likely have to prepare typically for a term of time. Living in a van can make you be stronger and better ready for your everyday challenges.

[141]

After Living In A Van - What To Do

Living in a van is no easy task, and often times individuals do not examine the things they would like to do after they adhering to a minimalist lifestyle. So much time is spent on preparing, yet hardly any thought is contributed to your recovery strategy. While focusing on residing in a small space is essential, you should also examine the things you would like to experience afterwards. There is no doubt you would feel more positive about

[143]

yourself upon achieving your aspiration to adhering to a minimalist lifestyle.

Make sure to permit time to recover from living in a van. If you are just starting at living in a van, then it is best to take it slow. To reduce the time it would take to bounce back on track, here are a few methods to help yourself recover.

After living in a van, make sure to take what you learned into your future situations and benefit from them. You ought to also make sure to continue living simple. That would completely help you recoup all of the energy that you put forth on living in a van. In addition, be really mindful not to judge yourself. That can impede your overall recovery. In addition, make sure you do not resort back to old habits that may no longer serve you.

After living in a van, you might feel burned out physically and intellectually. After investing six months preparing for your specific goals, it is typical to want a bit of time to rest. During the time you are within your period of relaxation, it is a sensible idea to consider the things you might want to achieve next. While you do not need another specific objective in mind, it is a sensible idea to have a starting idea where you hope to go next. Please remember, do not bounce into something new all at once. Make sure you are totally recovered so you can see to it that you are truly ready. You can potentially harm yourself by pushing too hard. This is the reason that moment of rest is so essential.

This is a benefit of permitting yourself to rest. Then create your plan. It may become difficult to keep preparing without a clear-cut objective in mind. Once you produce a solid plan, you ought to begin right away.

You do not need to get right back to preparing once you accomplish your aspiration. Put in a few moments to recover. Just bear in mind not to strain your body so you maintain the momentum to carry out your other ambitions!

Common Questions About Living In A Van

By now, you should be cognizant of the preparations you should take to live in a van. If you think of a question that hasn't been addressed, do not be alarmed. Following are a handful typical questions that come up with living in a van:

Is it viable to live in a van economically?

For most people, it is viable to live in a van economically. It is pointless to invest a lot of money preparing to live in a van. Following are several instructions to manage costs.

- Don't spend money on expensive meals. You can save a lot of money by investing in a cooler to contain your less costly store bought food. Practice eating foods that are easy to prepare and which are a healthy choice. This will keep you healthy and sound while living in a van.

- Budget your travel expenses. Buy gas when it is down price-wise and travel less to save on gasoline/petrol. Also, ensure that you are not buying things you do not need (too much will clutter up your van and invade your small living space).

- Get oil changes at regular intervals and learn how to fix minor repairs. You can learn about your vehicle by watching YouTube videos, through online resources, and by talking to knowledgeable professionals. The more you can do for yourself, the less you'll spend hiring out other people's services.

One other question that frequently comes up when people are preparing to live in a van is relating to the typical "rules" to recognize while residing in a small space. Following are a handful of guidelines to bear in mind:

- While camping out, Remain alert to your surroundings. This would be calibrated to anything out of the ordinary that may pose a threat.

- Typically, traveling afar is essential when residing in a small space. This would foster a sense of safety by having a plan 'b' to fall back on.

- As you hone in on reducing possessions, be sure to Be content with less things holding your back from living a freer life. This would feel free to exist without the responsibility of ownership.

You have successfully begun the first step toward living in a van by reading more about it. Most likely additional questions could come up and another way you can benefit yourself is by approaching this objective with a friend that might have similar objectives.

At times the "buddy system" is a good solution while approaching a desire that requires a thrifty and wealthy nature. While you would ultimately live in a van by yourself, it makes sense to join someone upon the same quest to discuss challenges as they pop up. Be mindful to select like-minded friends and avoid individuals who are spender or spendthrift, because such people might pull you away approaching your objectives.

Remember all the questions you had responded to just a bit ago?

Do you want to reduce your cost of living?

Do you want to save money?

Do you want to be free to travel and live where ever you desire?

You have responded "yes" to the questions that determined you had the most effective nature to do well at living in a van. Choose a friend that might also answer "yes" to these particular questions because such people would also be inclined to do well at living in a van.

Have fun living in a van!

The End.

Take A Course

You may be done with this book; however, you're never done learning. I have put together some courses on various subject matter which may assist you with your learning.

I'm guessing you want to hone your communication and persuasion skill, and the good news is you can when you take one of these courses. Take a few moments to check out some of our offerings. You may be surprised by what you learn.

If you'd like to get an updated list of courses offered at indirectknowledge.com please connect with us at www.indirectknowledge.com. We're always giving away free goodies too, so make sure you join our emailing list.

Here are some of our course offerings:

To learn more about covert conversational hypnosis so you can persuade anyone by merely having a 'seemingly' normal conversation with them please check-out:

www.learnconversationalhypnosis.com

If you are a professional sales person you may also be interested in my sales hypnosis course.

To learn more visit:

www.howimakesales.com

Want to learn how to get wealthy without resources (credit, money, friends, etc.) then check out:

www.howicreatewealth.com

[159]

About The Author

Bryan Westra is a noted speaker and master level hypnosis and NLP practitioner and trainer. He is an international bestselling author, Success Coach, and the founder and owner of Indirect Knowledge Limited—a training and publishing house.

To learn more about Indirect Knowledge Limited please visit:

www.indirectknowledge.com

To learn more about Westra's books please visit:

www.bryanwestra.com

To learn more about sales hypnosis please visit:

www.howimakesales.com

To learn more about hypnosis please visit:

www.howihypnotize.com

Learn Well; Live Well.

Course Notes:

Course Notes:

Course Notes:

Course Notes:

CPSIA information can be obtained
at www.ICGtesting.com
Printed in the USA
FSOW01n1036260117
30051FS